Thanks Mom

Joseph Lowry

Thanks Mom

Independently Published

Copyright © 2020, Joseph Lowry

Published in the United States of America

181031-758981.2

ISBN: 9798616005311

No parts of this publication may be reproduced without correct attribution to the author of this book.
For more information on 90-Minute Books including finding out how you can publish your own book, visit 90minutebooks.com or call (863) 318-0464

Here's What's Inside...

Introduction 1

Chapter One
Thanks Mom,
for Giving Me Life 4

Chapter Two
Thanks Mom,
for Your Spirituality 8

Chapter Three
Thanks Mom,
for Your Example of Compassionate
Service and Sacrifice 12

Chapter Four
Thanks Mom,
for Being Family-Focused 15

Chapter Five
Thanks Mom,
for Being a Patriot 17

Chapter Six
Thanks Mom,
for Your Wonderful Cooking 20

Chapter Seven
Thanks Mom,
for Your Focus on Good Nutrition 23

Chapter Eight
Thanks Mom,
for Your Supreme Example
of Refinement 26

Chapter Nine
Thanks Mom,
for Your Focus on Physical Fitness
and Conditioning 29

Chapter Ten
Thanks Mom,
for Your Love of Culture and
the Fine Arts 31

Chapter Eleven
Thanks Mom,
for Your Love of Travel 34

Chapter Twelve
Thanks Mom,
for Having a Great Sense of Humor 36

Epilogue 39

Dedication

To my angelic mother, Josephine Helen Cunningham Lowry, of whom there is no equal.

Introduction

If children are lucky in this life, we are blessed with a wonderful mother, and I was lucky. Before I tell you about her, I would be very remiss not to mention the other incredible mother figures in my life, whose presence at different times and places also richly blessed my life. The list of other mothers would, of course, first include my two grandmothers, Ethyl J. Lowry and Nelly Edith Cunningham. My recollections of them, their life examples, and the time I spent with them are truly special. Second would be my two aunts, Hazel Cunningham Gilliam and Ethyl Lee Lowry Chesser.

Third, of course, were the mothers of my closest friends as a child, teenager, and subsequent adult. These women were Eleanor Rogers, mother of Bill Rogers; Martha Moore, mother of Don Moore Junior; Gertrude Compton, mother of Philip Compton; Marie Peterson, also known as "Gran" Marie Peterson and mother of George

Peterson; and Barbara Meadows, mother of Rick Meadows.

Taking a prominent spot to the right of my mother was my wonderful and very loving mother-in-law, Raquel Sastre. She blessed my life both while living and through her beautiful daughter (and my exceptional wife of almost 45 years), Gladys Sastre Lowry.

All of these women had a profound influence on my growth and development. All of them were very loving and knew how to relate to boys. I knew their love for me was unconditional. These God-fearing women had a great sense of humor and knew how to have fun and how to make life fun for us. Why is this significant? Because of that, I believe they were more inclined to be kind, loving, patient, and persuasive in their efforts to mold their boys into good young men.

I feel a deep and abiding love and a profound appreciation for each of these women; I am grateful to God that all of them were placed in my life path, but above all the rest stands my mother. She was an angel. She raised five children; there were four boys, of which I was the youngest and one girl. Each of us was a challenge in our unique way. Like all women who choose to give birth, she put her life on the line to bring me into the world. She wasn't perfect, but she always did her best. On this point, I have no doubt whatsoever. She nurtured and cared for me as an infant, child, adolescent, and young adult. Her caring didn't stop there. It continued into my adulthood and until her death.

Her concern for me, her counsel to me, and her prayers on my behalf, as well as for my subsequent family, never waned, not one iota. She was a consummate daughter, sister, wife, mother-in-law, mother, aunt, grandmother, great-grandmother, and an elegant southern lady. The purpose of this book is a feeble attempt to recognize her and express my gratitude for all she has done for me. It is a direct reflection on the multitude of ways I see her loving and enduring influence in my life. I hope it will be a blessing in the lives of all who read it.

Chapter One
Thanks Mom, for Giving Me Life

I am eternally grateful that my mother chose to give me life. Having observed the sacrifices and devotion to childbirth and child-rearing exhibited by my wife, daughter, and daughters-in-law, I have been even more deeply moved to appreciate the sacrifices made by my mother. It is my opinion that the most unselfish gesture that can be made by any human being is that of creating life and then devoting all of one's days to the success and blessing of that being. Curiously, that can only be achieved by a woman, a mother. Thanks Mom, for giving me life.

My Early Childhood

I remember her making sure that I was given every opportunity to participate in a variety of different activities. I remember her as always being involved in my school. She was probably the room mother on more than one occasion. She was very diligent in communicating with my teachers and endeavoring to find out, if I fell short somewhere, what remedy needed. If I expressed an interest in anything, she was always ready to support me in that pursuit and to make sure that I had every resource available to succeed at it.

I can honestly say my mother never let me down. My mother never did anything that was a disappointment to me or that ever made me feel I was not the most important person in her life, though I think that's a widespread problem among most mothers. When you have four other children, I think it's a pretty unique ability to make one feel like the most important person. Now, some of my siblings might insist that I *was* the most important person in her life, but that, of course, is their perception. My mother and I had an extraordinary connection, an exceptional relationship, and nothing negative comes to mind regarding my relationship with her.

My mom had a great sense of humor, or at least the ability to find humor in almost any circumstance, whether it was embarrassing or something else. Laughter was not in short supply in our home. There was no lack of humor in our home.

Is She Your Wife?

Of course, beauty is in the eyes of the beholder, but my mother was a very beautiful lady. I recall when I was younger, probably around six years old, I was on a road trip with her and my older brothers, and somebody confused her as the wife or the sister of my oldest brother. He was 17 at the time, and she was already probably in her 40s by then. One time, she ordered her Thousand Island dressing on the side. The poor server brought the salad, and the dressing was on the side, but it was a dollop literally in the bowl on the side. We laughed and laughed. She was just a fun lady.

Eternally Devoted

There was a certain intensity in her devotion to getting things done. She was a pioneer, I would say, in eating whole foods or plant-based diets. You can Google the original pioneer in health food or healthy eating, a woman named Adelle Davis, who published the first books on this topic. Of course, as my mother embraced these philosophies, she got a wheat grinder and ground her wheat. Some of my fondest memories were of coming home from school to the smell of freshly baked bread, watching the butter melt on the bread, putting some honey on it, and eating it with a glass of milk.

She was a superb cook and chef, but she had this thing about health. I took who knows how many vitamin and mineral supplements. I recall drinking my orange juice with a tablespoon of brewer's yeast in it and powdered sea kelp. All of these things are acknowledged today as very healthy: vitamin C, vitamin E, vitamin D, raw honey, etc. I probably ingested my body weight several times over in healthy supplements growing up in that house, but she did it all out of love.

Jack LaLanne, who was a television pioneer in personal fitness, was a mainstay on her TV agenda. I don't recall that she watched any soap operas. That was never a part of our regimen in the house. She not only wanted to make sure she gave us a good life but a healthy life as well. It was never forced on us, but you just did it. She said, "Here, take this," and you did it because you knew she loved you, so maybe that's why I'm still here.

Chapter Two
Thanks Mom, for Your Spirituality

When I was growing up, I must admit that my mother's prayers seemed to last forever. Now as an adult with my own family and daily challenges, the value of prayer, and sometimes the length required to cover all the bases, has naturally created the need for more time to express to God both gratitude for my many blessings and to enlist His help in protecting and blessing the lives of those I love and those in need. Mom was a pillar of faith. A devout Christian and an active member of her church, she devoted countless hours to serving others in a variety of callings. She did so without ever uttering a single complaint or criticism. Her faith taught her and me that God is waiting, too, and will bless us if and when we do our part.

She was God-loving and firm in her faith, yet kind and gentle as she taught me about God. She taught me true principles from the Holy Scriptures about the life of Christ and His teachings and from other good books, wherever wisdom could be found about how to live a good life. She accompanied me to weekly and intra-weekly church meetings with perfect regularity. She made every effort to ensure that I would receive every available spiritual blessing. In short, she led the way by example.

Every Sunday

My father was raised a Christian but was not active in any faith. On Sundays, my father would be off to the country club to play a round of golf and maybe a few rounds of Gin Rummy, and then he'd be home for Sunday dinner.

My mother, on the other hand, would wake us up with a full breakfast for everybody. There were no Pop-Tarts. She cooked us a full breakfast, with eggs, bacon, toast, juice, and pancakes...the whole nine yards. Sunday was no different.

We'd get up and have breakfast; our clothes were always clean and pressed. We got suited up, so to speak, and went to church on Sunday morning. At that time, our church divided its services into two parts. We had a morning Sunday school, which was about an hour and a half, and then would be the evening worship service, typically between 6:00 p.m. until 7:30 or so. That was our day. She believed that the 10 Commandments said that the Sabbath day is a day of rest and to keep it holy, and you refrain from doing other things on Sunday. Whether it was our landscaper or whoever it was, there was no work done on our home on Sundays, and we didn't ask anybody to work.

Sunday was a special day. I remember that she was very active in serving. She served as the president of the women's auxiliary in the church for many years. She served as the president of the children's organization, called the primary, and she served as a teacher multiple times. She served as a local missionary, as well. Her faith was a very central part of her life, and she believed it. When I say I thought I was going to die of old age while she said her prayers, I'm not exaggerating. To a kid, anything more than, "We thank you for our food, amen," would take an eternity.

In retrospect, she was sincere and very humble. As such a person, she set an example that I still have not attained but strive to emulate. My mom's seeds of spirituality planted in me a firm foundation of faith. She believed that the United States of America was founded under the inspiration of God. Of course, that translated into a very strong sense of patriotism and a belief that the United States is a special place and has a special role to fill in the world in terms of preserving freedom. She taught me well.

When I was in high school from grades nine through 12, our church had what they call 'seminary,' which is essentially Bible study, every morning for an hour before school. When I was a freshman in high school, classes started at 7:30 a.m.

This required me to be up by 5 a.m., have breakfast, and at the church by 6 a.m. for this class with these other high school students, and then on to school by 7:30 a.m. That meant my mother was probably up at 4:30 a.m., again, preparing a full breakfast and then taking me to the church for this early morning class, which I did every year for four years going through high school, as did my sister.

I stand in awe of her example. Of course my wife Gladys, and I, did the same thing for our kids. I think having that example made a big difference in our doing it also.

Chapter Three
Thanks Mom, for Your Example of Compassionate Service and Sacrifice

Going back to my earliest recollection, my mother was actively engaged in the service of others. Cooking for and delivering meals to those who were injured, ill, or adversely affected were her common and regular activities. As I grew up, it became readily apparent that most of these acts were spontaneous on her part and rarely the result of any outside request. If there was a need, she filled it. If there was a pain, she soothed it. If there was sadness, she always had a smile and a kind word.

For Mom, sacrifice came easily, never with a grumble or complaint and never with judgment or criticism expressed regarding the intended recipients. She was a model of acceptance of others, whatever their station in life, and unconditional love for all of God's creatures. Thank you, Mom, for your perfect example of Christ-like kindness, gentleness, and love unfeigned.

After my mom passed, I would hear remarks about how she had done this or that for a needy family or someone who was sick. Growing up in the South at those times, in certain areas, there could be very strong racial bias. My father was born and raised in Georgia, and his bias was very strong. My mother, on the other hand, never said anything of a biased or prejudicial nature at all. I think that that played a very critical role in my growing up years, being very tolerant of other races and other faiths and other nationalities, whatever it might be.

I have never felt any prejudice at all. I feel that that went a long way to our raising our children that way. As they chose an associate or a friend, our advice to them was to choose people with like values. It makes no difference to us their color or their economic background or whatever. Just make sure that they possess the qualities that you strive for.

We had, as was customary in the south at that time, people who worked for us. One of our maids would drive me for my swimming lessons at the country club or wherever I needed to be. I loved these women, and they blessed my life. The gentleman who used to come and maintain and polish the floors and so forth was the janitor at my father's company. He's the man who taught me how to drive a manual shift, and I loved him dearly. When he died, I was away at college, and his death was very devastating to me. Again, I always observed my mother being very kind and very gracious with people of color in particular. I'm very appreciative of that perspective. It's a beautiful legacy that I've strived to pass on to my children as well.

Chapter Four
Thanks Mom, for Being Family-Focused

For Mom, everything was all about the family: family prayer, family home evening, family reunions, family trips, family history research, and nightly family dinner together. It didn't stop there. Whenever we could include the whole extended family, she would do everything in her power to bring everyone together from time to time. Most importantly, from her, I learned that you never give up on family, no matter where they are, who they married, or what they've done.

Never Give Up on Family

You just never give up or throw in the towel regarding the members of your family. It's no small wonder that I emerged into adulthood with similar inclinations. Thanks Mom. Your example has served my family and me very well.

I was fourth of five boys, and then my sister came unexpectedly at the end. My third oldest brother, Mike, was a very sweet, good person, but for reasons, I somewhat understand (and will not elaborate on here) was very conflicted for most of his life. As a result, he did some things for which he had to spend time in federal prison. He never killed anybody or assaulted anyone, but today, we might refer to it as white-collar crime. Nevertheless, he received the judgment that was appropriate for what he did.

My mother persisted. As a small boy, I can recall sitting in the back seat of my mother's car, driving my brother to the psychiatrist. This happened in 1954 or 1955.

She just didn't stop. Ultimately he died at age 48, and I know that she felt at his death that she had failed. I wouldn't be surprised if that sadness contributed to her early demise. There were a few other family tragedies that occurred, which also probably had a lot to do with it, but she never gave up on my brother. She loved him, and I loved him. He was a great guy.

Chapter Five
Thanks Mom, for Being a Patriot

In Mom's eyes, the United States truly was "America the Beautiful." She fully believed and instilled in me the belief and conviction that our forefathers, notwithstanding their human weaknesses, were inspired by Divine Providence to band together and establish a nation where freedom, justice, and liberty for all prevailed. She reaffirmed those beliefs in me at an early age by taking me to the various locales of early American history, thereby ensuring that their names and sacrifices were firmly embedded in my heart and mind forever. She was a member of the Daughters of the American Revolution, having identified those of our ancestors who fought in the Revolutionary War.

From my youth and throughout the present day, I still feel an emotional tinge when I hear the National Anthem sung or see the American flag waving in the breeze. I am grateful she saw fit to share her personal feelings with me. Thanks Mom, for being a patriot.

History Came Alive

As I mentioned previously, she firmly believed, and reaffirmed that belief through conversation and otherwise, that the United States was a special place. When I was probably age 11 or 12, we traveled up to Williamsburg, Virginia, and from there on to Pennsylvania, as well as a number of other places of particular note during the colonial period, such as the battlefields of the Revolutionary War, and historic sites about the Civil War, and other places. I was blessed to be able to see and experience things like Arlington Cemetery in Washington, DC, and to visit the halls of Congress and the White House. We visited The National Archives to see the Constitution. We got to visit all of these really important shrines and memorials in Washington, DC, showing Jefferson, Washington, Lincoln, etc. If there was a place to see, she took me there. If there was something to learn, she made sure that I learned it.

She was very active politically in terms of promoting candidates she believed in and contributing financially to their success; parties in our home to meet the candidates, and other things like that were not unusual. She was very active and lived her patriotism.

Gentle Patriotism

Today, we have a lot of rancor and hatred between the opposing parties. In those times, people had differences, but they could laugh together and appreciate one another. I miss that. I really appreciate having experienced that because I know that it's possible. People just have to do it.

Chapter Six
Thanks Mom, for Your Wonderful Cooking

Much has been said and still is, about the wonders of true Southern cooking. Mom was a consummate cook and baker. Every dish was a masterpiece in both appearance and taste. I have so many memories of helping her in the kitchen, licking the batter bowl clean, or eating a raw cookie and bread dough. Of course, the best part was sampling the finished product fresh from the oven. To my closest recollection, when I was around nine or ten years old, she purchased a wheat grinder and began grinding her own flour for bread, cakes, pies, et cetera.

Many days, I would come home from school to the aroma of fresh-baked whole wheat bread. I would pour myself a tall glass of cold milk, sit down at the kitchen counter with a nice, thick, warm slice of fresh bread, apply the butter, and then top it off with maybe some apple butter or guava jam. What a treat! Every evening, the family would gather together for dinner and then commence savoring Mom's creation of the day, always delicious, always well-balanced, and always a manifestation of her love for us and whoever else might be visiting.

The aromas from her kitchen called your senses to attention, and your taste buds danced for joy in anticipation. Thanks Mom, for teaching what good food really should taste like and how it should be presented.

My Favorite Dinner

I would say leg of lamb was probably my all-time favorite, with mint jelly and fresh string beans, maybe creamed corn or a baked potato. There were just numerous things. She made a killer London broil, and a perfect filet.

Back in those days, the *Good Housekeeping* magazine would have on the cover these sumptuous pies and dishes which almost looked like today's *Williams Sonoma* catalog, let's say, with these fantastic things. It's such a great memory to recall everything she cooked as if it came right out of a catalog or a magazine somewhere. Her meals were so delicious and beautifully presented.

My Favorite Dessert

There were so many wonderful things Mom made, but I loved her blueberry cobbler. Fresh blueberry cobbler probably was my most favorite dessert, although I just turned 70, and the sweetest recollection of my birthdays is that she would make me an apricot cake.

There would be pieces of apricot in the cake batter, and then there would be apricot jam in the layers. Then the frosting would be like a buttercream apricot icing (mmmmmm... buttercream apricot icing).

I've had a local baker prepare an apricot cake for me a couple of times, and she is outstanding, but my mother still made the best.

Chapter Seven
Thanks Mom, for Your Focus on Good Nutrition

After reading chapter six, you may be inclined to wonder if this chapter is at odds with it, or even out of order, but read on, and I think your questions will be answered. The acquisition of the wheat grinder came along when Mom became interested in proper nutrition and the use of vitamin and mineral supplements to augment our diet. She was at the cutting edge of the nutrition revolution as she read and implemented much of the advice of then-guru, Adelle Davis; who even today, is still revered as a great mind, and forerunner in healthy diet and proper eating.

A Healthier Me

Not to be outdone and also coming into his own in the '50s was fitness and diet guru, Jack LaLanne. Mom also bought and read his books, watched his TV programs, and endeavored to apply his thoughts on nutrition in her own life and ours. There was also another name of interest to her that I recall, Howard Inches, who was an actor and a devotee of healthy diet and nutrition in those years. As I recall, my father didn't buy into the whole nutrition idea, but he supported Mom in her efforts. As my sister and I were still minors, we were brought along for the ride. In retrospect, I am grateful for those early glimpses into the value of consuming, where and when possible, natural and unprocessed foods, whole grains, fresh fruits and vegetables, and vitamin and mineral supplements.

I vividly recall mixing brewer's yeast and/or ground sea kelp into my orange juice, along with a neat little pile of various pills, all with the purpose of producing a healthier me, designed by the person who loved me the most: my mom. There's no question in my mind that because of those early influences of my mom and her inclusivity of us in her quest to eat better and enjoy better health, that her spirit lives on in my efforts to "Go thou and do likewise." Thanks Mom, for always giving me the best in nutrition.

I forgot about the wheat germ. We had wheat germ in everything; and Postum too! Postum was a powdered beverage, consumed either hot or cold, and made from toasted grains. She would drink Postum instead of coffee, in harmony with our religious belief, The Word of Wisdom.

Eat, Eat, Eat

I don't know that this applies to healthy eating but bear in mind that I had three older brothers, big eaters. My oldest brother (he just passed away) was 12 years older than I am. About the time when I was five or six years old, he was almost out of high school. My mother got frustrated because, no matter how big of a complete breakfast she cooked in the morning, these three teenage guys were never satisfied. She ended up serving them steak every morning. They had steak, eggs, pancakes, toast, bacon, and gravy on the whole thing. Finally, they were placated. That seemed to satisfy them. She was determined. It was like she wasn't going to let anybody second-guess her efforts of trying to make sure everybody was well-fed.

Chapter Eight
Thanks Mom, for Your Supreme Example of Refinement

On this point, I cannot begin to say enough, nor elaborate sufficiently, about my mother as a true Southern Lady, raised in the Southern tradition of elegance and good manners. Mom taught all of us the importance of neatness and cleanliness in our appearance. All of her sons were taught to open the door for a lady, to assist her with her seating, and to be attendant to a lady's needs. In other words, she taught me how to be a Southern Gentleman.

As for table manners, there were no shortcuts here, either. No elbows on the table. Sit up straight. Chew with your mouth closed. Don't talk with food in your mouth. Don't take large bites. It was not uncommon for us to eat our dinner on fine china while using sterling silver flatware.

All of these factors combined to increase the probability that we would leave the nest properly prepared for the best life could offer. When it came to her clothing, she was always tastefully fashionable. She was never overdressed or ostentatious in her appearance, but supremely elegant. While her physical beauty was readily apparent, her manner of dress was always appropriate. Of course, her focus on being properly and tastefully attired bled over into how I needed to dress. As I grew into my teenage years, it was no small task to convince her that I could make those selections on my own. She finally acquiesced, and I was free to choose from then on.

Regarding home decorating, again, she exhibited fine taste in furnishings. Our home was beautifully decorated and a true showplace. As a comic aside, as children, she insisted we were not permitted to lie down on certain furniture in the formal living room for fear that the "oil" from our hair might stain the cushions. Needless to say, our heads did find their way to those cushions on numerous occasions whenever she was away from the house.

It's funny how we remember people from our past, and particularly Mrs. Oliver, the interior decorator my mother used. I recall her as being very nice yet somewhat distant in her manner.

I remember very well her station wagon packed full of samples of carpeting, wallpaper, wood finishes, and paint color samples. It was always fun to browse the array of possibilities. Thank you, Mom, for being an excellent example of good taste and refinement.

Chapter Nine
Thanks Mom, for Your Focus on Physical Fitness and Conditioning

As I have already alluded to in prior chapters, Mom was always striving for good health and fitness. In my childhood era, there were few gyms, if any. Those that did exist were devoted entirely to men's bodybuilding and weightlifting. There were no gyms that catered to women. Given her constant drive for self-improvement and achievement, it is no small wonder that, in addition to her penchant for healthier eating, she also was keen on the idea of physical conditioning, a la the '50s and '60s, and The Jack La Lanne Show.

I also remember her reading his books. For those times, especially, he was a cutting-edge fitness guru who espoused daily exercise and conditioning along with healthy eating. He would brag throughout his life that he had never even eaten a cracker. He directed his lifestyle advice primarily toward women and thus found his way onto my mother's radar.

Another one of my early recollections of my mother's entrée into the world of fitness was her purchase of the Stauffer machine, which reportedly slimmed one's waistline by placing a sandbag on the stomach of the user while they lay down on the device while the mechanized rocking undercarriage would move back and forth, thereby shaving fat and pounds off your hips and waistline.

I must confess to having experienced this phenomenon as a boy whenever my mother wasn't present. Being a slender, thin little boy, I could never attest to whether it actually worked, but my mother seemed to think it had some redeemable value in her fitness regimen. While I, to this day, have never exhibited any athletic prowess per se, she was very diligent in assuring that I had the opportunity to participate in youth football at the Coral Gables Youth Center.

Perhaps those early exposures to fitness were responsible for my interest in and adherence to an act of personal fitness regimen later in life. At least, I'd like to think so. Thanks Mom, for setting the example throughout your life by striving to stay fit and look good.

Chapter Ten
Thanks Mom, for Your Love of Culture and the Fine Arts

Somehow, when I was about seven or eight years old, I was taking organ lessons from a very wonderful, loving, and patient teacher, Mrs. Catherine Crowder. My mother, as far as I can surmise, thought that I would be a great organist one day. This introduced a full church organ into the music room of the foyer in our home. At about nine years of age, I was playing the organ for the weekly Thursday afternoon children's activity day at our church. These lessons continued until I was about 14 years old.

In addition, I would play the piano for the junior Sunday school lesson each Sunday. On occasion, I would fill in for our regular Sunday services. At age 14, I actually filled in for the ailing organist at the nearby Catholic Church in Coral Gables, where I lived. While I played, the spirit of playing never really caught hold of me enough to push me beyond 14 when boys have other interests on their minds. My mother's faith in me, her dedication to transporting me here and there for lessons and performance, combined with the knowledge I acquired about music, harmony, and tonality, all of this has paid big dividends throughout my life.

After leaving the organ behind, I expressed an interest in taking voice lessons, so she located a well-known voice teacher and proceeded to take me to lessons with him. Alas, I didn't care for his personality, and that ended the vocal training.

As if all this motherly attention and dedication were not enough, she purchased season tickets to the Metropolitan Opera series in Miami and began taking me to all of their performances, as well as those of the local philharmonic and visiting orchestras and soloists. In addition to all of this, if we visited New York, Washington DC, or any other major city, you can be sure we would visit the art galleries and attend the concerts wherever available.

In retrospect, as I am writing this tribute, it has become even more apparent that her desire to ensure my understanding of the arts was stronger than steel. The nicest part of all this is that my memories of being with her through all these activities are happy and pleasant. Thanks

Mom, for exposing me to the fine arts and for your many personal sacrifices in doing so.

Jet-Setting Mother and Son

When I was 11 or 12 years old, jet airplane service had just been introduced from Miami as a direct flight to New York. My father said, "We're going to New York." That was a big deal. Back then, flight attendants wore white gloves, and you ate your meal on a tablecloth and a tray. You wore a coat and tie when you flew on the plane. It's just a very vivid recollection.

When we got to New York, of course, we saw several Broadway musicals and plays; whatever happened to be playing at that time. I specifically remember seeing *The Sound of Music* with Mary Martin, who was a wonderful and very talented actress. If Broadway plays or musicals came to Miami on tour, we would go see those as well. My mother introduced me to musical theater, which I still love until this day.

Chapter Eleven
Thanks Mom, for Your Love of Travel

My dad never seemed to enjoy traveling, per se, unless it was tied to golf or some social or business activity. My mother, I am confident, would've traveled the world over if only Dad had shared that inclination. Nevertheless, she was diligent in taking us, her children, to places of historical and patriotic significance. We were also exposed to the beautiful mountains in the western part of the USA and other areas of our country. These early experiences created in me a love for varied landscapes and natural settings. As a result, I have an appreciation for a variety of geography and landscapes. Thank you, Mom, for awakening in me a love and appreciation for nature in all its forms and varieties.

My Favorite Trip

When I was six years old, Disneyland in California was set to open. It was 1955. My mother planned a trip with us, four boys. In a Pullman car, we took the train cross-country to the West and saw all of the country going west. Just traveling there was really quite the experience.

In California, of course, we went to Disneyland, which was this new creation. It was a wonderful memory. There was another place called Knott's Berry Farm, and we went to the movie studios and ate at the Brown Derby. We saw the Walk of Fame. Everything you could have seen, we did.

Before leaving California we went up into Yosemite. We moved on to Wyoming and Yellowstone. We saw geysers, hot springs and the Grand Tetons. It was really a magical trip. We got to see all of the national parks and about everything else of note that you could see that was open to the public. It was quite a trip and never to be forgotten.

Chapter Twelve
Thanks Mom, for Having a Great Sense of Humor

Mom had a way of finding humor in almost any situation and was not shy about sharing it. No matter the circumstances, be it a car accident, missed plane flight, or a family problem, she always kept her sense of humor, and that is a special gift. That gift of humor, which she gave to me, has served me well in countless situations throughout my life. I was grateful there was no lack of laughter in our home. Thanks Mom, for your wonderful and resilient sense of humor.

The Car Accident

This is a great story. When I was 15 years old, at that time in the State of Florida, you could only drive during daytime hours with an adult seated next to you in the passenger seat. It was called a 'restricted driver's license.' My mother and my aunt, her sister, were very involved in researching our family history and genealogy, so they proceeded to take my sister and me with them on a trip into Tennessee, in that area where my mother's ancestors come from.

One morning, my mother said, "Would you like to drive?" I said, "Of course." There was a light rain. As we were going down this little country highway, I don't know if it was my fault or if the road was slick, or a combination of the two, but we went around this curve that was over a bridge, and the car slid through the guardrail off the bridge and down into this gully.

We were probably 25 feet down. It wasn't into a canyon or anything, but it was significant. Of course, the car was totaled. The police came, and this was just outside of Knoxville, Tennessee. The vehicle was taken into Knoxville, where we went to the dealership; my father was on the phone negotiating to buy a new car. We had been there probably about four or five hours, and I noticed that my mother was still wearing her raincoat. I said, "Mom, it's not raining in here. Why are you wearing your raincoat?" She smiled and said, "I wet my pants." Of course, the excitement of the accident if you were in the passenger's seat, you'd be scared to death. She kept her raincoat on and never said anything.

We all laughed about that, and as we looked back on it, it was funny. Of course, there were no seat belts back then, so it was, "Hang on; we're going down the hill! Brace yourselves!" At least we had eaten a good breakfast that morning.

Epilogue

You may be wondering what prompted me to write this book. Well, the desire to do this was born out of an early morning observation that I had one day while driving home from the gym. As I rounded a corner, I noticed a young mother waiting for the city bus, with a toddler in tow and a younger baby in a stroller. I was profoundly moved, almost to tears. It prompted me to begin reflecting on all of the multitudinous inputs, touches, and points of contact that combine to make us who we are, but more profoundly, the woman who would give all she had to bring me into the world. She would make sure I was adequately fed and clothed, protect me from danger, cry herself to sleep worried about the choices I was making, and even lay down her own life and worldly comforts so that I might live and find happiness.

One day, as a challenge, I also attempted to list all that my mother had done for me and realized I was not capable of such a daunting task. Since that morning and even before my mother passed away, long before I was ready to let her go, I reflected on the many times I should have and easily could have picked up the phone, called her and told her, "Mom, I love you so much. And I will be forever in your debt for all the sacrifices and the love you have given me." How I wish she were here now for me to tell her just that and so much more.

In conclusion, I give to you, the reader, this challenge. If your mother is living, call her and tell her how much you love her. If she's far away, tell her how much you miss her. Then make sure you see her as often as you can.

If there are unresolved issues that have negatively impacted your relationship with your mother, then jump over the issues and follow the challenge in the foregoing paragraph. Take that burden off your back. Set it aside and love your mother. If your mom is deceased, then sit down and write her a letter. I wish I had written this book and presented it to her before my mother died so unexpectedly. You could even use the outline of this book as a guide. Then, share that letter with your family so they can feel a portion of what you feel and be blessed by your doing so.

I would hope, going forward in my family and yours, that we would always demonstrate respect, kindness, gentility, and respectful behavior towards the mothers in our family, all the women in our family no matter their age, and all women everywhere as well. May we recognize the profound influence of good women in our lives and their ongoing positive influence on the survival of our society as we know it and would like for it to be. This is my prayer,

I Love you Mom,

Joe

Made in the USA
Middletown, DE
10 January 2025